MEET THE MANAGER

20 THINGS YOU DIDN'T KNOW YOU DIDN'T KNOW ABOUT SEAN DYCHE!

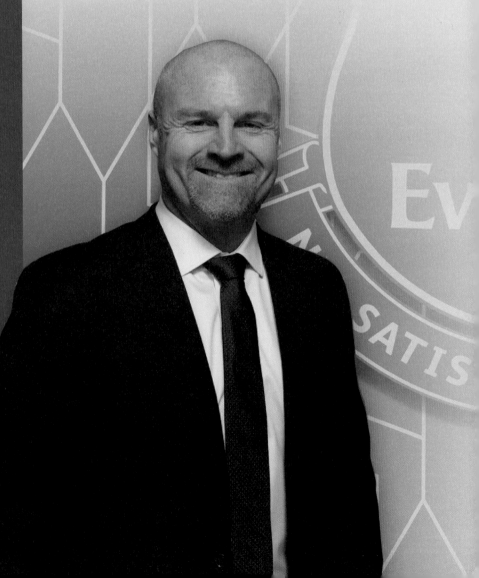

Everton
1878
NIL SATIS NISI OPTIMUM

■ Sean Dyche was born on 28 June 1971 in Kettering, which is in Northamptonshire.

■ He was a youth team player at Nottingham Forest in the 1980s when the legendary Brian Clough was the manager.

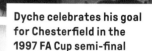

Dyche celebrates his goal for Chesterfield in the 1997 FA Cup semi-final

■ He never quite made the first team at Forest and in 1990 he signed for Chesterfield.

■ In 1997, Chesterfield very nearly became the first team from the third tier to reach an FA Cup final. Dyche scored one of the goals as they took a 2-0 lead against Middlesbrough in the semi-final but sadly the tie ended 3-3 and 'Boro won the replay.

■ At 2-1 in the first game, Dyche's team-mate Jon Howard hit a shot that crossed the line, but the referee and the assistants ruled, incorrectly, that it hadn't gone in, and the 'goal' didn't stand.

■ After more than 250 appearances for Chesterfield, Dyche left in 1997 to join Bristol City.

■ At the end of his first season with Bristol City, they were promoted to the First Division (now the Championship).

■ The Robins were relegated back to the third tier straight away and in 1999, Dyche signed for Millwall.

■ In 2000/01 he won another promotion with Millwall back to the second tier and in the following season they lost in the First Division Play-Off semi-final to Birmingham City.

■ After Millwall, Dyche had a three-year spell at Watford and then he ended his career with Northampton Town, with whom he won another promotion.

■ After hanging up his boots, he returned to Watford as the coach of their Under-18s team.

■ In 2009 he became the Hornets' assistant manager, and two years later he was appointed as their manager, succeeding Malky Mackay.

■ Dyche left Watford in 2012 and joined the England Under-21 coaching staff on a temporary basis.

■ In October 2012 he was asked to become Burnley manager after Eddie Howe left Turf Moor to return to Bournemouth.

■ Within two years, Dyche had steered Burnley to promotion to the Premier League.

■ They were relegated back to the Championship but in 2016 they returned to the top flight as Champions.

■ In 2017/18 Burnley finished 7th in the Premier League and qualified for the Europa League. The club had not been in Europe since the 1966/67 season!

■ During his time with Burnley, Dyche won two Premier League Manager of the Month awards.

■ In January 2023, he was appointed as manager of Everton.

■ His first game in charge was against the Premier League leaders, Arsenal, and Everton won 1-0!

Shouting instructions during his Watford days

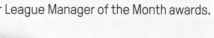

Winning the Championship with Burnley

MEET THE STAFF

IAN WOAN

Born in Heswall, Merseyside, lifelong Evertonian Ian Woan started his playing career with his boyhood club but never managed to break through to make a senior appearance. He drifted into non-league football and his big break came when Brian Clough signed him for Nottingham Forest from Runcorn FC.

Nearly 40 years later, he eventually returned to the Blues to become Sean Dyche's assistant manager. The pair first met when Woan was a young professional at Nottingham Forest.

Between 2012 and 2022, Woan spent almost a decade at Burnley, helping the club to secure promotions to the Premier League, as well as earning European football with an impressive seventh-placed top-flight finish.

Prior to that, he had worked with Dyche as assistant manager of Watford between 2011 and 2012. The move came after Woan had cut his teeth with various coaching positions at West Ham United, Portsmouth, Nottingham Forest, Rushden & Diamonds, and Swindon Town.

Between 1990 and 2000, Woan played over 250 games for Forest, before then moving to Barnsley. Later in his playing career, he had two spells in the United States and turned out for Columbus Crew, Miami Fusion and New York-based Syracuse Salty Dogs.

STEVE
STONE

MARK
HOWARD

Before becoming a coach, Steve Stone enjoyed an impressive playing career at the top level, featuring for Nottingham Forest, Aston Villa, Portsmouth and Leeds United, as well as England.

Stone started out at Forest in 1989 and, after overcoming three broken legs, managed to establish himself as a vital player, helping the club win promotion to the top flight and later playing in the UEFA Cup. Stone made nine senior appearances for England, and was included in the Three Lions' squad for Euro 1996, playing three times in the tournament.

In 1999 he moved to Aston Villa, where he played in the 2000 FA Cup Final.

Stone later represented Portsmouth and Leeds United before retiring in 2006.

He then moved into coaching and worked for Newcastle United from July 2010 to June 2015 in a variety of different roles at youth and first-team level.

In 2018, he joined Burnley as the new manager of the Under-23s, before stepping up to work alongside Sean Dyche in a first-team coaching role.

Mark Howard joined Everton to support the Sports Science team, having previously worked with Sean Dyche for almost a decade at Burnley.

At Turf Moor, Howard operated within the role of Head of Sports Science. In his field, he is one of the most experienced practitioners in the country, having gained a wealth of experience at several top-flight clubs throughout his career.

In 2001, he joined Bolton Wanderers and went on to spend more than six years as the club's First Team Strength and Conditioning Coach. Between 2007 and 2008, he held similar roles at Newcastle United and Fulham, before joining Blackburn Rovers in July 2008 as Head of Sports Science.

Howard worked at Blackburn for more than four years before departing to join Dyche at Burnley in 2013 to operate again as Head of Sports Science.

He stayed on at Turf Moor after Dyche's departure but subsequently left in September 2022.

PICKFORD'S PENALTY POSERS

1

SAVED ☐   SCORED ☐

2

SAVED ☐   SCORED ☐

3

SAVED ☐   SCORED ☐

4

SAVED ☐   SCORED ☐

Welcome to my PENALTY QUIZ!

On these pages you'll see twelve photographs of penalties given against Everton during my time with the club.

All you have to do is guess which ones I saved and which ones were scored.

I'll give you a clue – there are six of each!

ANSWERS ON PAGE 62

10

5

SAVED ☐ SCORED ☐

9

SAVED ☐ SCORED ☐

6

SAVED ☐ SCORED ☐

10

SAVED ☐ SCORED ☐

7

SAVED ☐ SCORED ☐

11

SAVED ☐ SCORED ☐

8

SAVED ☐ SCORED ☐

12

SAVED ☐ SCORED ☐

BONUS QUESTION Here's something you don't see very often – I am about to TAKE a penalty! Do you know what game it was? (Clue – it wasn't an Everton game!) And did I score?

JAMES TARKOWSKI

GETTING TO KNOW
DWIGHT MCNEIL

BIG
INTERVIEW →

In action for Burnley

What was the first team you played for?

I was at Manchester United's Academy when I was 5-years-old and then went to Burnley when I was 14.

Would we know any of your United team-mates?

James Garner was at United with me – he was in the year below me. Angel Gomes was there too, he is now at Lille in France, and Brandon Williams.

Which team did you support as a child?

Manchester United.

How often did you watch your dad play?

Every week when they were at home.

(Dwight's dad, Matty McNeil, played professionally for Macclesfield Town and Stockport County)

When did you make your Burnley debut?

2018 against Bournemouth at home. I came on as a substitute and I replaced Aaron Lennon, who used to play for Everton!

When did you score your first goal?

The season after (2018/19) against West Ham at Turf Moor. We were 1-0 up when I scored at the far post from an Ashley Westwood cross. It was only my second start and we won 2-0.

What were your first impressions of Sean Dyche?

That he was an honest, hard-working manager who knows what's required. He's a great gaffer.

What was it like to play for England in the Toulon Tournament in 2019?

It was a great experience because it's always great to represent your country, although it was disappointing not to get as far as we wanted to. We were in a group with Japan, Portugal and Chile and we didn't qualify for the knockout stage.

Who else was in that England squad?

It was a good group to be fair. We had Reece James, Trevoh Chalobah, Marc Guehi, Eberechi Eze, Eddie Nketiah, Joe Willock, Conor Gallagher. Ben Godfrey was in and around the squad I think, but he didn't go to the tournament.

Can you remember when you first played at Goodison?

Yes I can! It was for Burnley in May 2019 – the second-to-last game of the season. We lost 2-0 and Seamus scored one of the goals. Tarky (James Tarkowski) was in the Burnley team with me.

How proud were you to make your England Under-21 debut against Slovenia in October 2019?

Very proud. It's a massive achievement and what made it even better for me was that I was part of a really good team. Aaron Ramsdale, Tom Davies and Phil Foden were in the team, and we drew 2-2.

Was it an easy decision to come to Everton?

Yes, it was a no-brainer. The club is massive and as soon as I heard Everton were interested, I knew this is where I wanted to be.

What do you think of the Everton supporters?

They are so passionate, and you can tell that the club is a massive part of their lives. I want to do well for them as much as for myself.

What's been your most memorable match for the Blues?

Brighton away last season. We won 5-1, I scored two and had one go in off the Brighton goalkeeper. Everything about that night was perfect from a team and a personal point of view. In fact, it was probably the best game I have ever played in.

Try and describe the atmosphere during the Bournemouth win!

Before the game there were some nerves but there was also excitement and when we got over the line it was just amazing!

Who are your best friends at Everton?

Garns (James Garner), Patto (Nathan Patterson), Keano (Michael Keane), Lonners (Andy Lonergan).

Who's the funniest guy in the dressing room?

I'd give it to Patto!

Do you have any matchday superstitions?

I like to put my left side stuff on first – sock, boot. Probably because I'm left-footed!

What's the best goal you've ever scored?

I liked the first goal I scored in that 5-1 win against Brighton or the one against Crystal Palace at Goodison.

Who has been your toughest opponent?

Kyle Walker.

Do you enjoy any other sports?

I like watching cricket. I'm not very good at it, but I like watching it. I loved watching the Ashes last summer.

Which other sportsmen do you admire?

Well, I think Lionel Messi is the best footballer of all time. With regards to other sports I admire Usain Bolt.

Lionel Messi – Dwight's favourite footballer

A goal at Brighton

NEW KIT

FACE THE CAMERA!

Whenever a brand-new kit is launched, it's always a lot of fun (and occasionally a bit chaotic!) when we invite some of the players to pose in it for the release photographs.

Last summer, we invited Dominic Calvert-Lewin, James Garner, Nathan Patterson, James Tarkowski, Dwight McNeil, Vitalii Mykolenko, Jack Harrison, Jordan Pickford, Meg Finnegan, Gabby George and Claire Wheeler to a specially assembled studio in Liverpool and asked them to 'face the camera' in the new gear!

Nathan and Dwight wait for DCL to finish

Smile please! Meg Finnegan's turn

Gabby George sizes up the camera

Is Tarky trying not to laugh here!

One for the What's App group!

Clare Wheeler faces the camera

Looks like a full moon for Vitalii...

ist chilling! Jack Harrison njoyed it anyway!

Dwight thought it was funny anyway...

Who's next... Paper, scissors, rock will decide

New goalie kit for England's Number One

NAME THE
PLAYERS

ANSWERS ON PAGE 62

All these players played against Everton last season in the Premier League. How many of them, and their clubs, can you name? And be careful, some of them are wearing their away kit!

IDRISSA GUEYE

UNDER-21s
JENSON
METCALFE

Jenson Metcalfe was born in September 2004 and started at Everton when he was just five years old. He broke into the Under-18s team in 2020 and made his debut for the Under-21s a year later. In 2022 he signed a new four-year contract and will again be an important part of the Under-21s squad for the 2023/24 campaign.

INTERVIEW

When did you first start to play football Jenson?

I was four years old when I first started kicking a football about in my back garden in Wigan. When I was five, one of the Academy coaches, Paul Bennett, came into my school to do a PE session, which included a game of football, and after the game, he asked me if he could have a word with my dad. I was brought along to the training ground the next day! I remember seeing Ross Barkley training on the next pitch. Liverpool asked me to go in as well, but I was never going to do that!

So we take it you're an Evertonian!

Yes! I've always been an Evertonian and would come to the games. All my family are the same. I always liked watching Nikica Jelavic and Romelu Lukaku.

Despite still being a teenager, you've been at Everton a long time. To go from the under-6s team to the under-21s takes a lot of commitment.

Yes, it does, and it's been hard work. My dad helped me a lot. We used to get the bus to training at times because we didn't have a car. But I had belief from the beginning that I had a chance. The coaches would always say that they hadn't seen many players who could use both feet like me.

What was it like when you played for the under-18s?

It was tough because I was younger than them, but the lads were great and supported me and helped me. I have always tended to play for age groups older than me and it's a good way to learn. You mature quicker as a player, being around older players.

Paul Tait and Keith Southern

22

You suffered an anterior cruciate ligament injury in 2022, which must have been very difficult to deal with?

It was devastating for me, and I was gutted. Everything was going so well for me and obviously I wasn't expecting to be badly injured. I recalled what my teachers had told me at school – that I may get a bad injury that could end my career and so I needed to keep up with my education. I made sure I did that, and I did quite well at school. I was good at English, and I could put a story together, but I wasn't as good with numbers.

Is the mental side of being injured just as tough as the physical side?

Yes, it is. Some days you feel better than others because it's not always straightforward. You can come in and the knee feels okay but the physio will say 'no, it's not quite right yet' and you feel it's a bit of a setback. It was nine months between my operation and my first session back on the grass.

What was your first tackle like when you came back?

You've just got to grit your teeth and get through it. After the first one, the rest feel a lot better! Last season was a long one for the Under-21s with lots of games but when the season ended, it was only just starting for me. I felt I'd got my form back quickly. That was important for me because I was questioning what I was going to be like when I eventually got back playing. But it was fine when it happened, although I knew I had to just tidy up my play in a few areas. I also had to get up to the speed of the games but after being out so long, I expected that.

When did you first get the chance to train with the first team?

It was when Carlo Ancelotti was the manager. One of the first-team players was unwell and so I got a shout to come into Finch Farm and train with the first team. Carlo didn't speak to me much, but it was a great experience.

Under-21 players often get asked to join in training with the first team to make up the numbers or even up the numbers. Things can change by the hour but it's good because it makes you feel more a part of it.

As an Evertonian, what's it like to play at Goodison Park?

It doesn't feel real! Even when we played there with no fans during lockdown, it was just like a dream. Just to have played at Goodison is a story to tell future generations. But you have to quickly get used to the surroundings and concentrate on the game.

Last season was the first for the under-21s manager Paul Tait and his assistant Keith Southern...

Keith had worked with some of the younger lads and Paul knew most of us from the Under-18s so they both knew what we could do, which helped them and it helped us. I've been lucky that I've always had good coaches at Everton.

Who is your favourite current player?

I always say Sergio Busquets, who has recently left Barcelona for Inter Miami. Not many people would say him but when he was at Barca, I just wanted to be him. Whenever I watch games on the television, I always pay attention to whoever is in my position, and I watch closely at what they do. I was on the bench last summer in a couple of friendlies and I watched what Idrissa Gana Gueye was doing.

Sergio Busquets

BLUES YOUNG DUO WIN THE EUROS!

Everton's James Garner and Jarrad Branthwaite were key members of the England Under-21 squad that won the European Championships in Georgia in the summer.

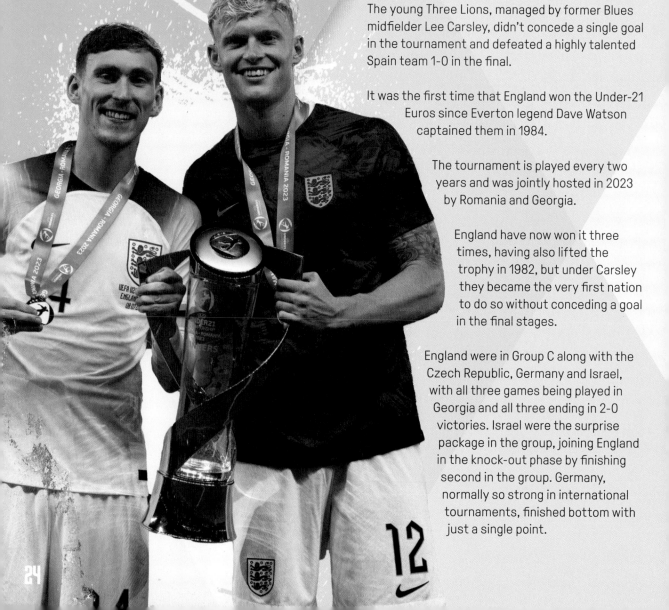

The young Three Lions, managed by former Blues midfielder Lee Carsley, didn't concede a single goal in the tournament and defeated a highly talented Spain team 1-0 in the final.

It was the first time that England won the Under-21 Euros since Everton legend Dave Watson captained them in 1984.

The tournament is played every two years and was jointly hosted in 2023 by Romania and Georgia.

England have now won it three times, having also lifted the trophy in 1982, but under Carsley they became the very first nation to do so without conceding a goal in the final stages.

England were in Group C along with the Czech Republic, Germany and Israel, with all three games being played in Georgia and all three ending in 2-0 victories. Israel were the surprise package in the group, joining England in the knock-out phase by finishing second in the group. Germany, normally so strong in international tournaments, finished bottom with just a single point.

In the quarter-final, a goal from former Everton winger Anthony Gordon was enough to defeat Portugal and then Israel were comfortably despatched in the semi-final – England winning 3-0.

The final against Spain was played in the Adjarabet Arena in Batumi, which is the second-biggest city in Georgia. In front of 18,498 spectators, a goal from Liverpool's Curtis Jones was enough to bring the trophy home. Goalkeeper James Trafford, who after the tournament joined Burnley from Manchester City, was the big England hero, saving a 99th minute penalty and then reacting quickly to also block the follow-up effort.

The England team that won the final: James Trafford (Burnley), James Garner (Everton), Max Aarons (Norwich City), Levi Colwill (Chelsea), Taylor Harwood-Bellis (Manchester City), Emile Smith-Rowe (Arsenal), Curtis Jones (Liverpool), Morgan Gibbs-White (Nottingham Forest), Anthony Gordon (Newcastle United), Angel Gomes (Lille), Cole Palmer (Manchester City).

Garner played in all six England games and Branthwaite played a starring role in the group victory against the Germans.

The 2025 European Under-21 Championship will be staged in Slovakia and by the time you read your Official Everton Annual, the qualification groups will already have started. England are in Group F alongside Ukraine, Northern Ireland, Serbia, Azerbaijan and Luxembourg.

CHART THEIR PROGRESS HERE...

Date	Opponents	Score	Scorers
11/09/23	Luxembourg (away)		
12/10/23	Serbia (home)		
16/10/23	Ukraine (away)		
18/11/23	Serbia (away)		
21/11/23	Northern Ireland (home)		
22/03/24	Azerbaijan (away)		
26/03/24	Luxembourg (home)		
06/09/24	Northern Ireland (away)		
11/10/24	Ukraine (home)		
15/10/24	Azerbaijan (home)		

FINAL GROUP TABLE

Position	Team	Points
1		
2		
3		
4		
5		
6		

ALL-TIME PREMIER LEAGUE APPEARANCES

There are six players with Everton connections in the all-time Premier League appearances Top Twenty.

Leading the way since the formation of the Premier League in 1992 is Gareth Barry, who made 652 appearances for Aston Villa, Manchester City, Everton and West Bromwich Albion. 131 of those Premier League outings came during his time with the Blues.

Fourth on the list with 609 is our former manager Frank Lampard, who accumulated his tally with West Ham United, Chelsea and Manchester City.

Two places beneath Barry is the late, great Gary Speed, who joined Everton from Leeds United in 1996. Speed played 535 times in the Premier League for Leeds, Everton, Newcastle United and Bolton Wanderers.

Also in the all-time top ten is former Everton captain Phil Neville, who played 505 games, winning six Premier League titles for Manchester United along the way. Neville's 242 Premier League appearances for Everton leave him 8th on our own all-time list.

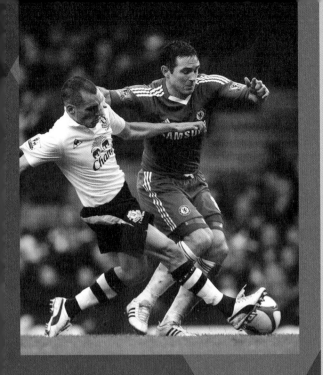

TOP 20
PREMIER LEAGUE APPEARANCES

The other two ex-Everton stars in the Premier League all-time Top Twenty are Wayne Rooney (17th with 491) and Sylvain Distin (19th with 469). Distin has played more times in the Premier League than any other outfield foreign player. Rooney is 3rd in the all-time Premier League goalscorers list behind Alan Shearer and Harry Kane.

The only other Everton player in the all-time goals Top Twenty is Romelu Lukaku.

1.	GARETH BARRY	652
2.	RYAN GIGGS	632
3.	JAMES MILNER*	619
4.	FRANK LAMPARD	609
5.	DAVID JAMES	572
6.	GARY SPEED	535
7.	EMILE HESKEY	516
8.	MARK SCHWARZER	514
9.	JAMIE CARRAGHER	508
10.	PHIL NEVILLE	505
11.	RIO FERDINAND	504
12.	STEVEN GERRARD	504
13.	SOL CAMPBELL	503
14.	PAUL SCHOLES	499
15.	JERMAIN DEFOE	496
16.	JOHN TERRY	492
17.	WAYNE ROONEY	491
18.	MICHAEL CARRICK	481
19.	SYVAIN DISTIN	469
20.	PETER CROUCH	468

* Up until the end of last season

MEET JACK HARRISON

Jack spent seven years with Manchester United's Academy before crossing the Atlantic to play college soccer.

His first professional team was New York City in the MLS.

His team-mates during his time in New York included former Everton manager Frank Lampard, Spanish legend David Villa and Italian hero Andrea Pirlo.

In October 2017, he made his debut for England Under-21s against Scotland.

In January 2018, Jack joined Manchester City (a sister club of New York City), but he never played a first-team game.

He was loaned out immediately to Middlesbrough.

Jack then spent three consecutive seasons on loan at Leeds United before making the move permanent in 2021.

In the summer of 2023, he joined Everton on a season-long loan.

Can you name these former Everton players who, like Jack Harrison, also played for Leeds United...

ANSWERS ON PAGE 62

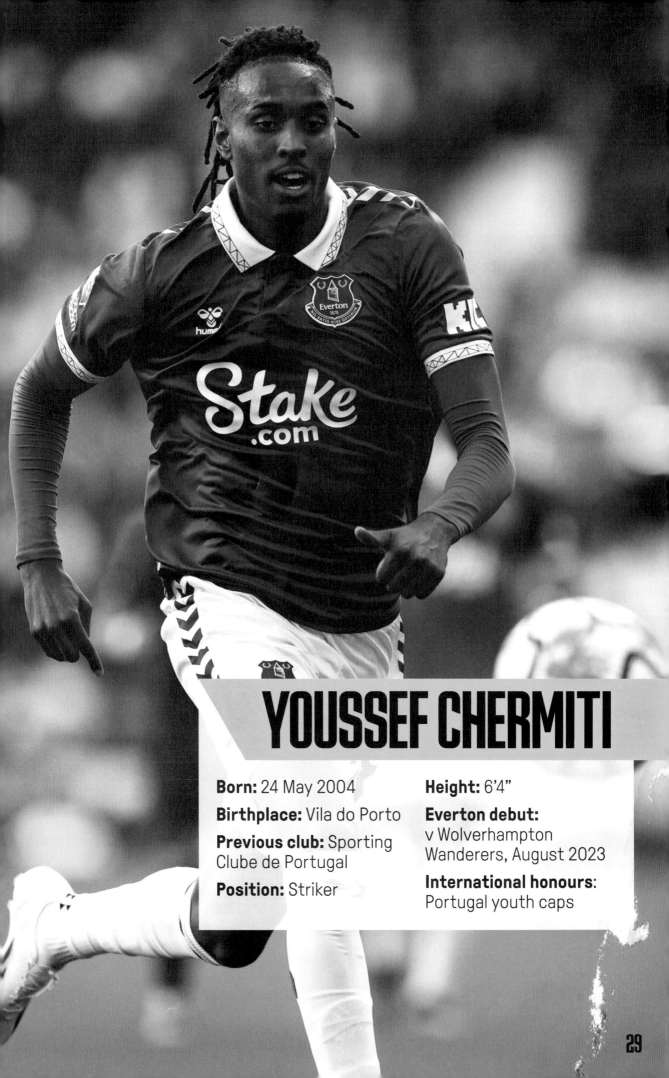

YOUSSEF CHERMITI

Born: 24 May 2004

Birthplace: Vila do Porto

Previous club: Sporting Clube de Portugal

Position: Striker

Height: 6'4"

Everton debut: v Wolverhampton Wanderers, August 2023

International honours: Portugal youth caps

SPOT THE BALL

ANSWERS ON PAGE 62

Here are two action shots from Everton's pre-season friendly match against Stade Nyonnais last summer. However, as you can see, we've added a few extra balls to each photograph! See if you guess the correct ball in each picture.

PREDICTIONS

By the time you read your 2024 Everton Annual, the new season will have already started. However, can you predict where all the bits of silverware will end up?

Guess who will win the top prizes and then when the season finishes, get your Annual off the shelf and see how you did!

You could even challenge your friends to do the same and see who gets the most right!

COMPETITION	2022/23 WINNERS	2023/24 WINNERS
PREMIER LEAGUE	MANCHESTER CITY	
CHAMPIONSHIP	BURNLEY	
LEAGUE ONE	PLYMOUTH ARGYLE	
LEAGUE TWO	LEYTON ORIENT	
NATIONAL LEAGUE	WREXHAM	
CHAMPIONS LEAGUE	MANCHESTER CITY	
EUROPA LEAGUE	SEVILLA	
EUROPA CONFERENCE	WEST HAM	
FA CUP	MANCHESTER CITY	
LEAGUE CUP	MANCHESTER UNITED	
SCOTTISH PREMIER LEAGUE	CELTIC	
WOMEN'S SUPER LEAGUE	CHELSEA	
WOMEN'S FA CUP	CHELSEA	
EVERTON'S TOP SCORER	DWIGHT McNEIL	

TOTAL SCORE ..../14

MEET NATHAN PATTERSON

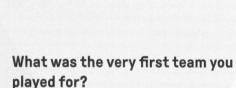

John McGinn - the best

What was the very first team you played for?

My boy's club team in Scotland, which was called Rossdale.

Were you a Rangers supporter as a kid?

Yes I was! My dad was a fan so he got me into supporting Rangers and I would go to the games with him.

Have you always been a full-back?

No, when I was younger I used to be a winger! When I started playing 11-a-side, I was moved to right-back to try it. I did well and really enjoyed it and I've been there ever since.

Who were your favourite international players when you were at school?

Barry Ferguson and Alan Hutton. They were both good players who stayed in the national team for a long time.

What school subjects were you good at?

PE...and that's about it really!

When did you first represent Scotland?

When I was selected for the Under-16s.

Brighton away last season

And when was your full senior international debut?

It was a pre-camp game before the 2021 Euros away to Luxembourg. I came off the bench to replace Stephen O'Donnell. My first Scotland goal was in a 2-0 win away to Moldova later that year.

What's it like listening to 'Flower of Scotland' before the games?

It's class, especially at Hampden Park when there's a full stadium. You can feel the pride from the fans, and from the players, and it really gets you hyped before the game.

Describe the Scotland fans in three words!

Just three words! Wow! Let's go for 'Loud, passionate...and Scottish!'

Who would you say is the best Scotland player you've played with?

I would say John McGinn for the influence he has on the team. He's a huge part of the squad and the fans love him.

Did you ever play in an Old Firm game and if so, what was it like?

Yes, I did and I loved them! Obviously being a Rangers fan, it was great to play against Celtic. They are the type of games you want to play in because they mean the most and if you can get a win, there's no feeling like it.

Did you always want to play in the English Premier League?

I think it's probably every young player's dream. When the opportunity came along to join Everton I didn't have any second thoughts.

Who are your best pals in the Everton dressing room?

We all get on great and there's a really good togetherness in the squad, which shows when we're out on the pitch even when times are tough. You can see that we are all fighting for each other.

How helpful has Seamus Coleman been?

He's been top! The first time I walked through the door, he was the first person to come up and speak to me. He said that he was looking forward to working with me. I enjoy being alongside him every day in training and learning as much as I can from him because he's a top, top player.

Describe the Goodison Park atmosphere when it's rocking!

It's crazy! It's unbelievable, especially the derby game and the last game of the season.

What's been your most memorable game in an Everton jersey?

Either the Merseyside derby or the win away at Brighton & Hove Albion when we played really well.

Who's been the toughest opponent you've ever played against?

Kaoru Mitoma of Brighton. He's small, he's sharp and he can go either way and can use either foot. He's clever as well. He's a great player.

Who would you rather not have to mark – Messi or Ronaldo?

I'll have to say Messi because he is just unbelievable. Obviously, I would also hate to have to mark Ronaldo but if I had to pick one to avoid it would be Messi.

International debut

HAT-TRICK HEROES

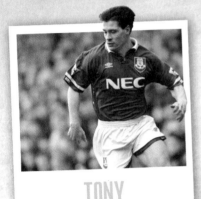

TONY COTTEE

Up until the end of last season, 14 Everton players had scored a hat-trick for the Blues in the Premier League.

In November 1996, Joe Royle's Blues thrashed Southampton 7-1 at Goodison Park with **GARY SPEED** netting three of the goals. The Toffees were 5-1 ahead by half-time so it could have been worse for the Saints!

The first one came in August 1993 when **TONY COTTEE** put three past Sheffield United to give Everton a three-wins-out-of-three start to the new season. Howard Kendall's Blues won 4-2 and the Sheffield United goalkeeper was, ironically, our current goalie coach Alan Kelly! Sorry Alan!

Cottee scored two Premier League hat-tricks for the club and the next player to get one was **ANDREI KANCHELSKIS** against Sheffield Wednesday at Hillsborough in April 1996. Everton won 5-2 and the goals took Kanchelskis's tally for the season to an impressive 16.

DUNCAN FERGUSON became the first player to score a hat-trick of headers when he did so against Bolton Wanderers in December 1997. It was the big Scot's only treble for his beloved Blues. Ironically, the only other player to have since scored a hat-trick of headers is Salomón Rondón, the former Everton striker, who did it when he was playing for West Brom.

Super **KEVIN CAMPBELL** was our next hat-trick hero. His goals helped Everton stay up in 1999 and in the last home game of the season he scored three times in a 6-0 win against West Ham.

DUNCAN FERGUSON

In February 2000, West Ham were on the receiving end of another Everton hat-trick – this time from **NICK BARMBY** in a 4-0 win at the Hammers old ground, Upton Park. Barmby later left Everton for Liverpool!

The first Everton hat-trick of the David Moyes era came from a most unlikely source. Defender **STEVE WATSON** was often pushed up front in an emergency, and against Leeds United in September 2003 he scored three times in a 4-0 win at Goodison. Not bad for a makeshift striker!

Nigerian international **YAKUBU** scored two hat-tricks for Everton – one in Europe and one in the Premier League. The Yak poached all three in a 3-0 win against Fulham at Goodison Park in December 2007.

ANDREI KANCHELSKIS

LOUIS
SAHA

WAYNE **ROONEY**

In February 2011, **LOUIS SAHA** became the first Everton player to score FOUR goals in a Premier League game. Saha, who scored our goal in the 2009 FA Cup final, put Blackpool to the sword in a 5-2 win.

The only player to score a hat-trick for Everton after coming off the substitute's bench is **STEVEN NAISMITH**. The Scot replaced Mo Bešić against Chelsea in September 2015 and then scored with his left foot, his right foot and his head in a 3-1 win. The perfect hat-trick!

In November 2015, **AROUNA KONE** scored a hat-trick in a 6-2 win against Sunderland at Goodison Park. Those goals represented half his complete Premier League tally for Everton.

Everton's all-time leading Premier League goalscorer is **ROMELU LUKAKU**. He scored three hat-tricks for the Blues, two of which were in the league. He scored all three in a 3-0 win at Sunderland in September 2016 and then netted four in a 6-3 victory against Bournemouth in February 2017.

WAYNE ROONEY didn't manage a hat-trick during his first spell at Everton, but he did it in his second. Rooney bagged three goals in a 4-0 win against West Ham in November 2017, with his third goal being scored from inside his own half of the pitch!

Prior to this season, the most recent Everton Premier League treble came from **DOMINIC CALVERT-LEWIN**, who achieved it against West Brom in September 2020. Sadly, there was nobody there to see it as the game was played inside an empty stadium during the Covid pandemic.

A record that will probably never be beaten...**DIXIE DEAN** scored an incredible THIRTY-SEVEN hat-tricks for Everton! Dean is also the only 18-year old to ever net a treble for the Blues.

In December 1893, **JACK SOUTHWORTH** scored TWO hat-tricks for Everton...in the same game! Southworth scored SIX goals in a 7-1 win against West Brom at Goodison. Southworth also had the distinction of scoring the first ever Everton hat-trick at Goodison Park! ■

STEVE
WATSON

STEVEN
NAISMITH

ROMELU
LUKAKU

WELCOME BETO

Birthdate:
31st January 1998

Birthplace:
Lisbon, Portugal

- Beto's full name is Norberto Bercique Gomes Betuncal and he was born in the Portuguese capital city of Lisbon on 31 January 1998

- On the day he was born, Everton drew 2-2 away to West Ham United – Howard Kendall was the manager.

- Beto started his senior career with an amateur team in Lisbon called Uniao Tires.

- In 2018 he signed for a Portuguese 3rd Division team called Olimpico Montijo, for whom he top-scored in his one and only season.

- His goalscoring exploits got him a move to the top division with Portimonense.

- He spent the 2021/22 season in Serie A on loan at Udinese.

- In April 2022 he scored a hat-trick for Udinese in a 5-1 win against Cagliari.

Scoring a penalty for Udinese

WHAT BETO SAID WHEN HE ARRIVED...

"It feels good to join Everton. I have always appreciated them as a club. Everton is a big, big club in the Premier League, well respected and has big history. It was easy to make this move.

When a club like Everton tries to buy you in January and then comes again in the summer, you feel like, 'Okay, they want me for real', so that made the decision easy for me as well. My idol, Samuel Eto'o, played here, too, which makes it even more special.

I can bring courage, I can bring confidence and I think my biggest thing is effort. I will always bring enthusiasm to the team and to our games. I feel like my style is a really good fit with Everton.

I am looking forward to getting started - today, right now. I know the team needs to score more goals and I will try to help with this. I love to score goals. I know we need this and I am here to help. I will always give my best to score goals.

It feels really good to be here and I want to make my mark. Let's do it."

- The following summer, the loan move was made permanent.

- In the 2022/23 season he scored 11 goals in Serie A.

- In October 2022 he was named in Portugal's preliminary 55-man squad for the World Cup in Qatar, but he didn't make the cut.

- In August 2023 he joined Everton!

- On his arrival at Finch Farm, Beto selected the squad number 14.

PREVIOUS EVERTON NUMBER 14s

John Ebbrell, Tony Grant, David Weir, Francis Jeffers, Idan Tal, Kevin Kilbane, James Vaughan, James McFadden, Steven Naismith, Oumar Niasse, Yannick Bolasie, Cenk Tosun, Andros Townsend

A previous number 14 - Steven Naismith

FA CUP QUIZ

ANSWERS ON PAGE 63

This Quiz has a twist! YOU are the Quizmaster!

Try these tricky FA Cup questions on a grown-up and see how they get on...

1 When Everton reached three successive FA Cup finals in 1984, 85 and 86 – which three teams did we beat in the semi-finals?

2 I was signed by David Moyes but only ever appeared in six games for Everton – one of which was the 2009 FA Cup final. Who am I?

3 Who was the only Everton player to miss his penalty in the 2009 semi-final shoot-out against Manchester United?

4 Which United player that day, later signed for Everton?

5 And which Everton player that day, later signed for Manchester United?

6 Who scored our first goal in the famous 1995 semi-final victory against Tottenham Hotspur?

7 Which team defeated us 9-8 on penalties in the 2015 3rd round?

8 John Heitinga and Leighton Baines scored our goals in a 2-0 win against which non-league team in the 2012 3rd round?

9 In 2021, we beat Tottenham Hotspur in the 5th round at Goodison – what was the final score after extra-time?

10 David Moyes' first FA Cup game as Everton manager was against the team that were 92nd in the league at the time! Bottom of the fourth tier. We lost! What was the team?

11 That game was also Wayne Rooney's first ever FA Cup tie. Did he ever score for the Blues in an FA Cup match?

12 After the famous 4-4 draw with Liverpool in 1991 – Everton won the second replay 1-0 at Goodison Park with a goal from which player?

Q9

Q8

Q10

Q11

DOMINIC CALVERT-LEWIN

EVERTON WOMEN

Brian Sorensen, Manager

The 2023/24 campaign is the 13th season of the Women's Super League and once again there are twelve teams competing for the title, currently held by Chelsea. The newcomers from the Championship this season are Bristol City who gained promotion and will replace Reading, who finished bottom of WSL last year.

Chelsea were pushed all the way to top spot last season by Manchester United, with the Londoners lifting the crown by just two points. It was Chelsea's fourth consecutive WSL title and their sixth in the last seven seasons.

Everton, under new manager Brian Sorensen, finished sixth with nine wins from their 22 league games. Sorensen, who hails from Denmark, will be looking to finish a bit higher this time around.

WALTON HALL PARK

Everton Women play their home fixtures at Walton Hall Park, less than a mile away from Goodison Park. It has a capacity of just over 2,000 and Sorensen and his players are hoping that supporters visit the venue in droves this season and really give the girls the backing they deserve.

2023/24 WOMEN'S SUPER LEAGUE FIXTURES

Sunday, 1 October 2023
Brighton & Hove Albion (home)

Sunday, 8 October 2023
Leicester City (away)

Sunday 15 October 2023
Liverpool (away)

Sunday 22 October 2023
Manchester United (home)

Sunday, 5 November 2023
Tottenham Hotspur (away)

Sunday, 12 November 2023
Chelsea (home)

Sunday, 19 November 2023
Bristol City (home)

Sunday, 26 November 2023
Aston Villa (away)

Sunday, 10 December 2023
West Ham (away)

Sunday, 17 December 2023
Manchester City (home)

Sunday, 21 January 2024
Arsenal (away)

Sunday, 28 January 2024
Leicester (home)

Sunday, 4 February 2024
Chelsea (away)

Sunday, 18 February 2024
West Ham (home)

Sunday, 3 March 2024
Manchester City (away)

Sunday, 17 March 2024
Aston Villa (home)

Sunday, 24 March 2024
Liverpool (home)

Sunday, 31 March 2024
Manchester United (away)

Sunday, 21 April 2024
Brighton & Hove Albion (away)

Sunday, 28 April 2024
Arsenal (home)

Sunday, 5 May 2024
Tottenham Hotspur (home)

Saturday, 18 May 2024
Bristol City (away)

MEET
MARTINA PIEMONTE

Birthdate:
7th Nov 1997

Birthplace:
Ravenna, Italy

She shares her birthday with Rio Ferdinand, David de Gea and Tinie Tempah!

A very talented footballer as a child, Martina signed a professional contract with Riviera di Romagna when she was just 14 years old.

Riviera de Romagna were in Serie A Femminile, the top division of Italian women's football, but the team no longer exists.

Martina was named in the Italy squad for the 2014 FIFA Under-17 World Cup in Costa Rica. The Italians reached the semi-final before losing to Spain but won the third-place play-off match against Venezuela.

After the tournament, Martina signed for San Zaccaria.

In 2014 she made her full international debut for Italy, aged just 16.

In 2016 she got a move to Hellas Verona, who were then in Serie A but are now competing in Serie B.

In July 2017, Martina left Italy to sign for Sevilla in Liga F, the top-flight division in Spain.

After one season with Sevilla, she returned home to join Roma.

But twelve months later she was back in Spain after joining Real Betis.

Move on another year and Martina went back to Italy to sign for Fiorentina.

She impressed so much in Florence that in 2021 she signed for the Italian giants of AC Milan.

Martina was in the Italy squad, wearing number 20, for the Women's Euro 22 Championships held in England.

The Italians finished bottom of their group, but Martina managed to find the net – scoring the consolation goal in a 5-1 defeat against France at Rotherham United's New York Stadium.

She was also in the Italy squad for the 2022 Algarve Cup – but she never featured in the final that the Italians lost against Sweden.

Last season, she scored 13 goals in 24 Serie A appearances for Milan.

In the summer of 2023, Martina signed for Everton!

Just after linking up with the Blues, Martina was off to the other side of the world to join up with the Italy squad for the FIFA Women's World Cup finals.

BUMPER QUIZ

ANSWERS ON PAGE 63

Here are some of the best international footballers in the world. Some of them, but not all, have played in the Premier League. How many of them can you name – and for extra points name the country and the current club team they play for.

....

....

....

Maddison

Emily & Henry

Leo

Shea

Melodie

Olivia

Eliza

Oliver

Owen

Olivia-Faith

Tobias

Jamie

Ava-Mae

Ruby

Teddy

Thomas

Conlan

Roman

Elijah

Amarlia & Melilah

Jax, Alyssa & Hallie

Zac

Jake

Joseph

Rosie

Millie

Ollie

Ethan & Dylan

Buddy

Rhys

Sophie

Leo

Ava

John

Everton
1878
NIL SATIS NISI OPTIMUM

FANS PHOTO GALLERY

Reuben

Isabella & Frankie

Mason & Noah

James

Leo

Elsie & Charley

Bobby & Freddie

Jacob

Alex & Harley

Roxi

Evie

Bella

Bobby

Hugo

Harvey & Ethan

Oliver

Jack & Alfie

Max & Bobby

Joe

Jacob & Joe

Billy & Phoebe

Noah, Joshua & Isaac

Maddison & Aubrey

Freddie

Noah and Thomas

Benjamin

Devon

Alfie

Ronnie & Kasper

Sonny

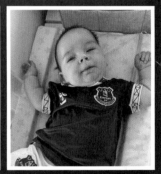
Max

Oliver

Noah

Everton
1878
NIL SATIS NISI OPTIMUM

49

GETTING TO KNOW
JAMES GARNER

Birthdate:
13th March 2001

Birthplace:
Birkenhead, UK

In action for England Under-21s

In September 2020 he signed a season-long deal with Watford.

That deal was terminated midway through the campaign and James switched to Nottingham Forest instead.

In October 2020 former Everton star Lee Carsley gave James his England Under-20 debut in a 2-0 win against Wales. Blues defender Ryan Astley was in the Welsh team!

James made his England Under-21 debut in a 2-0 European Championship qualifier against Kosovo at Stadium MK in September 2021.

He stayed at Nottingham Forest for another loan period for the whole of the 2021/22 campaign.

He helped Forest to promotion to the Premier League, playing in their play-off final win against Huddersfield Town at Wembley.

In September 2022, James left Manchester United for Everton.

He made his debut for the Blues in October 2022, replacing Seamus Coleman in the 75th minute of a Premier League game against... Manchester United!

James made 16 appearances for Everton during his first season at Goodison Park.

In 2023, James was in the England team that won the European Under-21 Championships.

James joined the Manchester United Academy at Under-8 level.

He was initially a centre-half before being converted to a midfield player.

He broke into the United Under-18 team during the 2016/17 season.

In 2018, James travelled with the United first team to the USA for pre-season, playing against San Jose Earthquakes and Real Madrid.

In 2018, he captained England at the UEFA Under-17 European Championships. Current Nottingham Forest boss Steve Cooper was the England manager.

England reached the semi-finals before losing on penalties to the Netherlands. Bukayo Saka was also in the Three Lions team.

In February 2019, he made his senior United debut, replacing Fred in the last minute of a Premier League game against Crystal Palace.

On loan at Nottingham Forest

A CAREER IN PICTURES...

Ashley Young joined Everton in the Summer of 2023. He arrived at Goodison Park having played for Watford, Aston Villa, Manchester United, Inter Milan and England. Here's his career in pictures...

1 Ashley joined Watford at the age of ten and went on to play more than 100 games for the first team.

3 In September 2006 his impressive early form in his first season as a Premier League player earned him an England Under-21 debut against Switzerland.

2 In 2006, he helped the Hornets to promotion to the Premier League, beating Leeds United in the play-off final.

COCA-COLA CHAMPIONSHIP PLAY OFF WINNERS 2006
WATFORD F.C.

4 But in January 2007 he left Vicarage Road to join Aston Villa – at the time he was Villa's record signing at £8m.

5 In November of that year, he made his full international debut when Steve McClaren brought him off the bench at half-time against Austria.

11 Three years later he was in the United squad that won the FA Cup. They beat Crystal Palace at Wembley after defeating Everton in the semi-final and Ashley replaced Marcus Rashford in the second half of the final.

6 In 2009 he was voted as the prestigious PFA Young Player of the Year.

7 His first senior England goal came during a 2-1 win against Denmark in Copenhagen in February 2011.

12 He played the full 90 minutes of the 2018 FA Cup final when United lost 1-0 against Chelsea.

13 Ashley was a regular in the England team that reached the semi-finals of the 2018 World Cup in Russia, including the semi-final loss against Croatia.

14 In January 2020, he left Old Trafford and joined Italian giants Inter Milan.

8 In June 2011, he moved to Manchester United.

15 In his first full season at the San Siro, 2020/21, Inter were the Serie A champions, making Ashley only the third Englishman to ever win the Italian top-flight title.

9 Ashley was part of the United team that won the 2012/13 title in Sir Alex Ferguson's last season as manager.

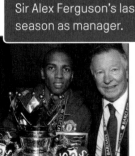

16 After that success, Ashley came back to England for a second spell with Aston Villa.

10 In 2012 he played in all four of England's European Championship matches. The Three Lions lost on penalties against Italy in the quarter-finals.

17 In July 2023 he signed for Everton!

53

GUESS THE KIT

Here are ten very close-up images of Premier League kits. All you have to do is guess which teams they are – but be careful because not all of the kits are the home version!

ANSWERS ON PAGE 63

WORD SEARCH

See how quickly you can find these eleven players, each of whom have scored more than 20 Premier League goals for Everton...

ANSWERS ON PAGE 63

A	S	C	O	T	T	E	E	Y	A
F	G	Y	E	S	T	A	R	E	L
D	X	A	O	U	M	H	O	N	L
L	U	K	A	K	U	A	O	Y	E
A	M	U	R	A	P	S	N	S	B
R	O	B	E	Y	U	N	E	E	P
T	R	U	T	G	M	C	Y	N	M
E	R	V	R	O	O	N	E	I	A
T	H	E	H	L	L	I	H	A	C
A	F	S	U	G	R	E	F	B	D

ARTETA   **CAMPBELL**   **LUKAKU**   **SAHA**
BAINES   **COTTEE**   **OSMAN**   **YAKUBU**
CAHILL   **FERGUSON**   **ROONEY**

ABDOULAYE DOUCOURE

NAME THE PLAYERS

ANSWERS ON PAGE 63

All these players have appeared in the Everton team in the Premier League in the last five years – can you name them all?

1

2

3

4

5

6

7

8

9

10

EVERTON IN THE COMMUNITY

Once again, 2023 was a really busy year for Everton in the Community. Celebrating its 35th Birthday, the Club's official charity continues to not only change lives but save lives too. The wide variety of programmes are unrivalled in sport and that's why Everton in the Community is the best charity in world football. Here are just some of the highlights...

Seamus Coleman loves to get involved...

...so does Amadou Onana

Jordan Pickford and Izzy Christiansen choose the winning design

Everton's Amputee team won their FA Cup

Ambassador Ian Snodin with some EitC staff at Kirkdale Station

WINNERS

James Tarkowski

Who better to give boxing lessons than Tony Bellew!

Toni Duggan presents some certificates

Seamus meets some of Everton Disabilty players

Ambassador Graham Stuart led an Everton team at the EitC Golf Day. Former Blues goalie Rachel Brown-Finnis was in his team. So was professional golfer Tommy Fleetwood's dad!

Andy Lonergan, Mason Holgate, Michael Keane and Billy Crellin also formed a team

Snods and former Liverpool goalie Bruce Grobbelaar launch the Annual Run for the 97

Sean Dyche called into the brand new People's Place centre

Everton's PFA Community Man of the Year was Dwight McNeil

Dwight was happy to play Santa!

And Snods was happy to meet a few more of them!

Seamus with some young participants

Under-21 players Jack Barrett, Joe Anderson, Matty Mallon and McKenzie Hunt help out

The EitC Veterans programme is brilliant. Here's Graham showing a few of them around Finch Farm

GETTING TO KNOW
ARNAUT DANJUMA

Birthdate:
31st January 1997

Birthplace:
Lagos, Nigeria

Celebrating a goal for Holland...

■ Three days later he scored his first international goal in a 1-1 draw against Belgium – managed by another ex-Everton boss, Roberto Martinez!

■ In August 2019, Arnaut decided to try the Premier League and he signed for Bournemouth.

■ Sadly for him, and for The Cherries, the team was relegated at the end of that season.

■ In April 2021, Arnaut was named as the Championship Player of the Month.

■ In August 2021, he was on the move again, this time to Villarreal in the Spanish La Liga.

■ He helped his new team to reach the semi-finals of the 2022 Champions League, scoring a vital goal against Bayern Munich in the quarter-finals.

■ In total, Arnaut scored six Champions League goals that season – the same number as Cristiano Ronaldo and Kylian Mbappe!

■ In January 2023, Arnaut joined Tottenham Hotspur on loan – and scored his only Premier League goal for them against his former side, Bournemouth!

■ Arnaut joined Everton on loan from Villarreal in the summer of 2023 and assumed the number 10 jersey.

■ Arnaut was born in Lagos, Nigeria, on 31 January 1997, and grew up in Holland.

■ He made his professional debut in 2015 for Jong PSV in the Second Division of the Dutch League. Jong are the reserve team of PSV Eindhoven.

■ From Jong, Arnaut moved to NEC Nijmegen, for whom he made his Dutch top-flight debut... against PSV!

■ In July 2018 he signed for Belgian side Club Brugge, for whom he made his Champions League debut.

■ Arnaut was first called up to the Dutch national team in October 2018 by former Everton manager Ronald Koeman and made his debut in a 3-0 Nations League win against Germany.

Playing against Real Madrid for Villarreal

QUIZ & PUZZLE ANSWERS

Page 10-11
Pickford's Penalty Posers!

1. Saved
2. Saved
3. Scored
4. Saved
5. Saved
6. Saved
7. Scored
8. Scored
9. Scored
10. Scored
11. Scored
12. Saved

BONUS QUESTION ANSWER
It was for England during a penalty shoot-out against Switzerland in the 2019 UEFA Nations Cup Third-Place Play-Off. And, of course, I scored!

Page 18/19
Name The Players

1. Diego Costa (Wolves)
2. Ruben Dias (Manchester City)
3. Danny Welbeck (Brighton)
4. Harvey Barnes (Leicester City)
5. Calum Wilson (Newcastle United)
6. Eberechi Eze (Crystal Palace)
7. Willian (Fulham)
8. Christian Eriksen (Manchester United)
9. Hugo Lloris (Tottenham)
10. Ben Chilwell (Chelsea)
11. Ben Mee (Brentford)
12. Jonjo Shelvey (Nottingham Forest)
13. Aaron Ramsdale (Arsenal)
14. Ollie Watkins (Aston Villa)
15. Jack Harrison (Leeds United)
16. Diogo Jota (Liverpool)
17. Danny Ings (West Ham)
18. Che Adams (Southampton)
19. Philip Billing (Bournemouth)

Page 28
Name the players

1. Jermaine Beckford
2. Ross Barkley
3. Fabian Delph
4. Aaron Lennon
5. Andros Townsend

Page 30
Spot The Ball